LETTERS TO MY DEAD

LETTERS TO MY DEAD

lisken van pelt dus

Three Bunny Farm Press

Dear you,

Naming

When you were alive I didn't really know
    what to call what I felt for you
but after you left I could name it –
        dragonfly, some days, or *Aldebaran*
        when the night is sharp –
something that wings after you,
        your scent and your aloofness,
        your hand to settle on.

These are the weeks when sunlight flees faster and faster
        until I both rise and go to bed
in darkness and live largely by the light
        of screens and CFL lightbulbs.
Something about the darkness brings the feeling back.
    I'll be working and it will land on me
        or bloom out of me –
        I'm not sure what comes first –
and suddenly I am naming again – *ocean*,
        or *basil* pricking my nostrils.
Then, gone.

Where will you be when you read this?
Where will you find the light to read it by?
What will it make you feel?

Love like Salt

It's fall now and the pandemic you
    never heard of is pounding our shores,
eroding us at all our weakest spots –
        our elderly, our poor, and our hubris.

I'm glad you're not here to see it
        but I want to know what you have to say.
I've been listening but haven't heard you.

I do know you would have kept
        doing what you could do.
And so do I, though it is piecemeal –
    a little raking, a burst of teaching prep,
    a new draft here and there
but not much revising, not much
reading, not much but what is preliminary –
        as in, front-loaded in effort and intention,
        as if insisting on a now that hopes
            for a future.

I've been cooking, for instance, which
    I suppose will please you, and you'll understand –
a making at which one's mortal being
    is fully present – scent of cinnamon, tang
        of rosemary, whisk of eggs frothing in a bowl –
and then it is appreciated and gone.

Or the lesson planning, same thing minus the senses,
    or the shopping lists I organize in order
        of my path through the grocery store.
Or this letter.

There's salt in it, and you –
        you're most likely near ocean,
so it should find its way. Let me hear
    how you're doing,
        what you have to say.

Rose Bush

Your rose bush still has blossoms
    though it has snowed once
and the trees around are nearly bare
    but for one strip of fire
       just at eye level.

I saw how hard it was for you
    to make peace with this constricted townhouse view
       large as your life was –

but you observed it closely, nonetheless,
    the trees when you died just beginning
to acquire leaves and the rose bush not yet budding.

Since then the scene has cycled fully and a half
       and here we are,
waiting once more for the rose to go to sleep.

What do you remember of going to sleep
    that last time? The peepers in the holding pond
were deafening. This year
       we hardly heard them.

Everything is quieter without you.

But you wanted me to keep writing
       so I am writing you a letter
as you used to do to me – a habit you acquired
    in days and places with few alternatives,
       and then kept up.
I have half a file cabinet drawer full
       of your letters full
of description and noticing –
    night-blooming cereus in your white-walled Jeddah courtyard,
    rare partridge on your oak knoll in Wisconsin,
    etched wrinkles in a hand at the Tate.

I should be more specific about the rose bush.
    There are two blossoms left
    and they are about to fall.

In Flight

I was thinking about the day we spotted a merlin
    and you told me they once were called lady-hawks
        because noblewomen used them
        to hunt skylarks.

Imagine. How could they hunt skylarks?

We spent a lot of time looking at the sky, you and I,
        or closing our eyes and gazing
    at the blood-orange of our eyelids
        lit by the sun –
good for our sight, you claimed,
            and I never wanted to check.

I liked to take your word for things.

Merlins have two speeds, you told me –
    zero or thirty-plus miles per hour.
Either waiting or killing.

Poor skylarks didn't have a chance.
Know where their name comes from?
        They sing in flight, rising and hovering
            to deliver their multitude of notes.

On the anniversary of your death
    I want to sky-write your name,
        a song hanging in the air, the air
        the color of your eyes.

Doing Good

En route to your old house, there's a stack
    of hay bales painted *Love Unity Respect*
        and then *Vote* smaller on the side –

and the crazy thing is that the first stack –
    which said *Biden Harris* – was burned down
and the farmer put this up instead.
He pitied the arsonist his son
        lost to a motorcycle accident.
Plus he believes in good, like you.

I mostly do, still. But damn there's a lot
    of stuff that people do –
        have done –
that, well, if it isn't evil, what else do we call it?

The other day another young Black man
    killed by police because
        he had a knife.

And the thing is –
        forgive me for repeating this phrase –
        but this is the work we are in now, you see,
        we have to dig under for the thing –
it's not an *incident*. It's not even pattern.

Sorry. Probably not what you want to hear about
    but you were always at home with the big questions.
Let me know what you think, okay?

Meanwhile, we're all staying busy, doing good.
Trying. Hope you're proud.

Election Day

It's Election Day and it's a doozy,
    everyone on both sides with so many toes
    and fingers crossed we're all in knots.

I'm thinking about *sides*
    and wondering how it looks from where you are,
the *other side*, we call it, across a barrier
    that doesn't seem so different from political divisions
        these days – almost impossible to imagine
thinking the other way.

Did the dissolution of your flesh
    dissolve in and out, is and is not,
    this side and that?

I don't want to feel adversarial. I swear
    I'm still motivated by love
    as you would insist of me.

When I walked the tracks today past the beaver pond
    almost nothing was stirring – only some robins
eyeing me askance as they lumbered
    from one branch to the next.

The walk was necessary.
For a brief moment I could be part
    of the stillness, something entire
without any concept of sides.

Probably don't have to tell you that.

But you'll appreciate the bare twig lying on my path.
One branching snaked in four tight switchbacks,
    delicate and elegant gray determination
    to grow however it could.

It would have been easy to carry home,
    almost weightless.
But I left it there – its tangles, its already deadness,
    the shape its life had taken.

The Whole Thing

Remember the article you shared with me
    about how crows gather around their dead?
They say now it's to detect threat
      but it sure looks like grief. Elephants, too,
      and jays, and chimpanzees.
    Why doubt it?

I thought of our exchange when I saw
    some video of tardigrades – the toughest creature
    on earth, they call them, extremophiles,
      able to survive even a vacuum or radiation –
anyway, I saw them nuzzling each other,
      embracing even,
        and it made me miss you.

We're missing a lot of contact right now,
    so maybe that compounded it.
Pandemic air-hugs only go so far
    and there's some part of spirit
    you just can't Zoom across the ether.

I wish I could send you everything –
    the video, and me – my spirit,
    our conversations,
    my body next to yours…
      But maybe you are glad
      to be done with body.

So I will send you what I can,
    out there somewhere, extremophile
    that you are – happiest at the edges.
I know you better than you know.

I'd love to hear back.
Try crows?

Advice

You always believed we were both exceptional
    but this kind of accolade
    depends on how you define goodness, doesn't it?

Now that you're dead
    and I will be one of these days
and neither one of us among those few
remembered beyond a hundred years –
        what do you advise?

There's been a quarantine on
    so I've been home a lot with more time
to make choices. And if goodness
involves results, scratch exceptionalism.
        I'm ordinary as piles on my office floor,
        dust gathering everywhere.

America, too, proving itself an exception
    to its own mythology, its rough spirit
splitting its soul like a log destined for fire.

You told me you'd lived a good life
        but by then you meant it
        had been good to you.
You took less credit than you used to.

Thanks for the advice.

Frost

Winter's coming. Most of the trees
    are bare and this morning for the first time
a heavy frost ghosted my car.

By the time I drove to the store
it had evaporated, but oh was the sky heavy
    over the cemetery on my way, bullet-gray.

And of course someone was being buried.
        It made me sad, seeing the lines of cars.

It's strange, isn't it, that we think of ourselves
        both as leaving and as being left,
    our bodies – *us* – giving up the ghost,
    letting it go, but also *us* the ghost, freed.

My friend Catherine took her husband's ashes
    on pilgrimage back to the places
    he had loved and left
        some in each spot, his *remains* remanded
to the bits of earth that witnessed him.

Soppy, a bit, but it gets at the seeing
        and the being seen that is living.

The frost didn't disappear. It just turned into sky.

I still see you.
I wanted you to know.

Humpty Dumpty

Your old friend Dominique wrote to me today,
    two days before your birthday.

Were you in love with her husband, a little?

We never quite had that conversation –
    the men we loved publicly,
    the men we loved privately,
        the women who loved those men.

Is love any easier now, free of body?

It was Dominique who gave us a copy
    of *Mots d'Heures: Gousses, Rames*, wasn't it?

        Un petit d'un petit…

As long as I am in body, I will be of yours.

Dominique sent pictures of her newest granddaughter
      watching Kamala speak on TV.

        Un petit d'un petit
        S'étonne aux Halles…

She couldn't visit them in Paris
    because of lockdown.

        Un petit d'un petit
        Ah ! degrés te fallent…

What else was lacking? What
    do you lack now?

Sometimes you would marvel at the similarities
    between your life and mine, our contradictions.
        For both of us – definition a kind of oscillation.
We average to some long-drowned city
in the Atlantic, to acceptable women,
to people of passable faith and faithlessness.

We bleed sweet and sour like citrus
        and complication, straddle walls uneasily.

Womanhood *another misdirection.*

I turn your memory over in my hands,
    like a secret,
        stroke it smooth.

    Happy birthday.

Keening

I dreamed last night you wrote me back,
  told me about the sky –
made of its own starlight, you said,
woven by filaments of something that sings –
    no, *keens*, you said – like love.

When I woke, I thought it was you
      who had roused me,
    but it was the sun instead.
Daylight savings has ended.

Did you know there is a field
        called helioseismology?
Waves like a heartbeat throb
inside the sun and when scientists listen
      they learn the shape of fire
    from its song.

This morning the song outside
  is from a neighborhood of leaf-blowers –
remarkably similar, in fact, to the recordings
      I found of the sun –
  whirring pulses and high sustained bells.
Moaning and keening.

But what else would you like to hear about?
      The kids had another scare –
    one of the twins pumping too much blood
from the placenta to the other –
    but they think they'll be okay.

Your death certificate says heart failure
    but I don't believe it.

Antelope

You were radiant in my dream last night,
   despite the usual travel hiccups
   compounded by the oddities of the unconscious –
     rock face to clamber down,
     and an airplane open to the sky
     with no place for the luggage –
you were just happy
     to get one more trip back home to London.

I'm trying to remember when your last real one was.
   It had been a while – five years? Ten?
   Maybe it was when you went to sell
your father's bronze antelope back to the gallery there.

A creature I'll never forget.

I love so much that you used the money
   for travel, en famille, in the grand style,
our own French river barge.
     It's Thanksgiving, so, once again, thank you.

How steadily the fields flowed past the canal.
Sometimes the charolais would lift
   their heads to watch us, but mostly
   they just kept grazing.

The lost-wax antelope, too, forever nuzzling the earth,
   expecting nothing of the next moment
but ready for anything.

In your final hours
     from where I sat by your side
   it seemed to be like this for you.
Like the antelope, that is, not the charolais.
   Wild, and ready.

I understand now how much you missed your father.

Weather Report

I miss reading about the weather
    wherever you were writing from –
        wind lashing the lake
        or wet pavement shining
        or sun perpetually baking your white courtyard.

Here? It's *unseasonably* warm – as if
        this weren't our new reality.
Bob even went golfing yesterday, fun but dear god,
        it's almost December.
    No snow yet – while hurricane upon hurricane
        lays into the south,
    splinters lives into matchsticks.

Tonight though, here, there is no denying it is beautiful.
    The full moon is haloed,
    and Jupiter and Saturn shine
        side by side like twins in the west.
When you died, they were far from each other –
    but Gemini, my constellation,
        was bang in the middle of the sky.

Bang in the middle of the sky at your bedside.
I thought you'd want curtains
        but I should have known better.

It was a small view but it held
    both woods and sky, and what you couldn't see
we reported – iced hillsides,
        roses blushing green.
When you lay awake in those late nights
you fixed your eyes on the stars burning.

Back here, the weather has been uneasy.

My grief won't keep to its season.

Missing

I heard about Jett. Most likely a fox?
    I'm sorry.
You loved a lot of cats in your time, but Jett –
        he was part you.

Now even that's gone.

Our local fox came by again the other day,
    cocky as anything – full daylight
        trotting across the yard.

I was happy to spot him –
        hadn't seen him in so long.
There's not much of any wildlife around lately.
    On a walk today I saw one small bird,
        and that's it,
    if you don't count humans.

Not that we've been seeing much of them, either,
    what with the virus and all.
Mostly I'm happy not to have to deal,
        but then I miss the hell out of them.
    Some of them (*smile*).

That's pretty much how Jett was, too, I recall –
        out and about
            until he wanted some loving.
Must have got that from you.

Tell me, does dying put an end to missing?

X

When I say it has been x years since you died
    x seems something other than a number,
time transformed into a globe I bounce around in,
        or a wind roaring in distant trees,
    so today x feels like an orange
        and yesterday it felt like arrows arcing.

This year is drawing to a close, one more year finished.
        As if it were something we accomplished.

The time-you-have-been-dead thing started right away.
    Hours measured in fingertips, months in ponds.
Now suddenly it is a lake, an orchard,
        a field of warriors with pierced shields.

You were ready at the end.
That seems like something to aspire to.
    Can we call it an accomplishment? I think so.

And now the New Year.
I'm lousy at resolutions, hate to pin myself down like that
        though I'm all for self-improvement.
    I know you understand,
            having housed your own competing forces.

Dot's counting now, by the way –
        one, two, four, maybe three, FIVE!
    Your kind of free-thinker.
    Soon she'll be two. Or x.

Anyway, happy new year.

In my Eyes

I ran across a passage today that called
    sorrow and joy
        the unmasked essence of each other
    and thought of course
        of losing and having you.

Unmasked means something new now
as masks have become an everyday,
    our public faces literally different
        from the ones we bare at home.
An odd sensation, seeing so little,
        trying to render joy with our eyes,
    read the sorrow in others'.

Maybe you'd find humor in the masks,
    call it the other side of despair.

It's hard to imagine you wearing one,
        though I guess if you were here, you would.
    When you had to, to protect others –
you were never afraid of dying yourself.

Was your transition as you believed it would be,
    just one thing melting into itself,
        as a river into the sea?

My sorrow was ocean when you died,
        like it was me you had flowed into.
        Like a dam holding our joy let go.

I hope you saw it in my eyes
when we were river together.

Lisken Van Pelt Dus was raised in England, the US, and Mexico, and now lives in western Massachusetts, where she is an award-winning teacher of writing, languages, and martial arts. Recent poetry can be found in *The Ekphrastic Review*, *Beltway Poetry Quarterly*, *Sky Island Journal*, and *Sand Hills Literary Magazine*. Her work has also been included in anthologies and craft books, and has earned several awards and Pushcart prize nominations. A full-length collection, *What We're Made Of*, was released by Cherry Grove Collections in 2016.

John Van Pelt was raised in Latin America, England, and the US, and has been privileged to enjoy a creative livelihood working for newspaper, digital media, and software companies. He now lives in central Maine, where he writes, edits, and designs for the indie publishing house that he and his partner operate alongside their sheep farm and fiber empire.

Made in the USA
Middletown, DE
18 May 2022

65842814R00020